AMERICAN PRESIDENTS

GEORGE WASHINGTON

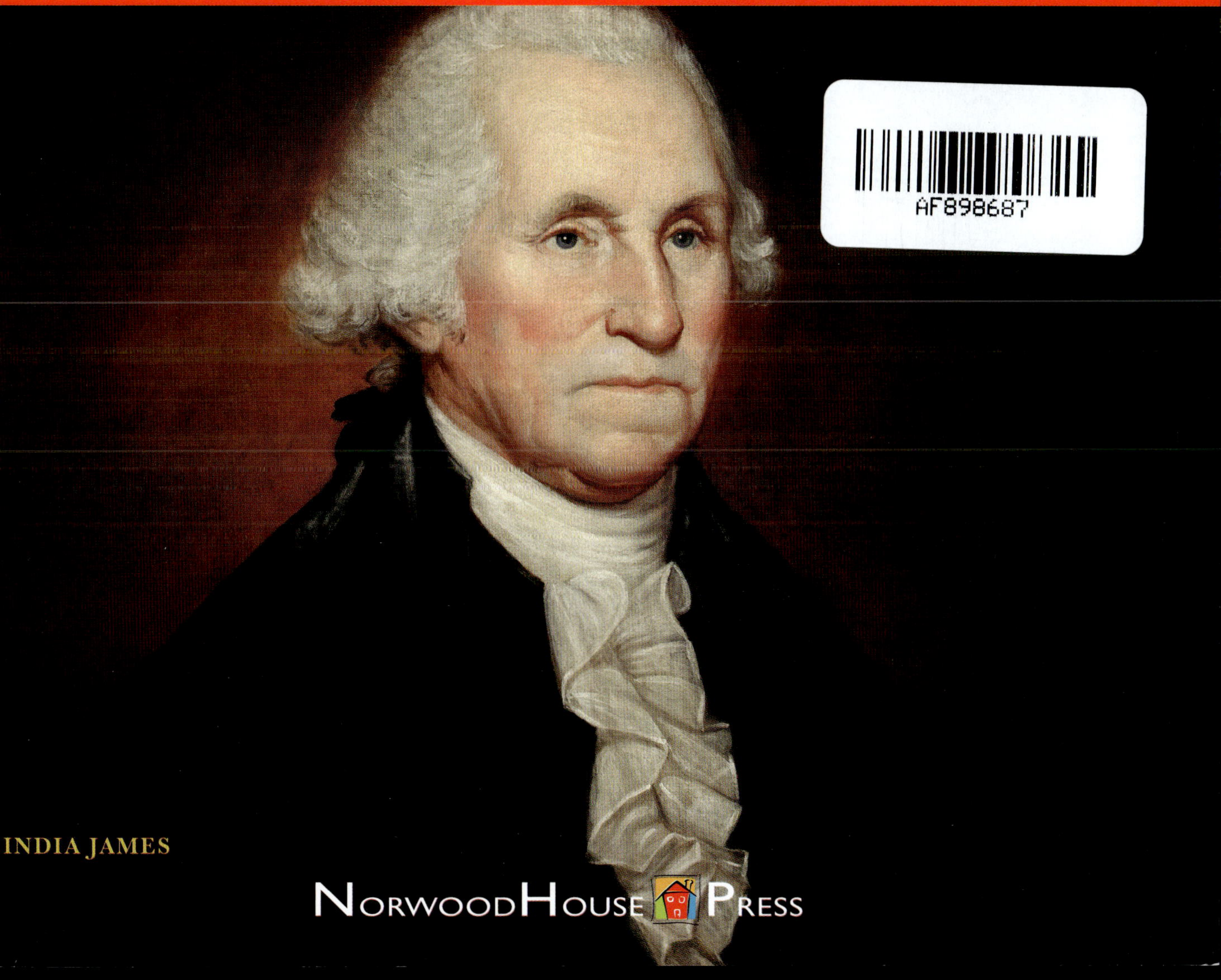

INDIA JAMES

NorwoodHouse Press

Cataloging-in-Publication Data

Names: James, India.
Title: George Washington / India James.
Description: Buffalo, NY : Norwood House Press, 2027. | Series: American presidents | Includes glossary and index.
Identifiers: ISBN 9781978579873 (pbk.) | ISBN 9781978579880 (library bound) | ISBN 9781978579897 (ebook)
Subjects: LCSH: Washington, George, 1732-1799--Juvenile literature. | Presidents--United States--Biography--Juvenile literature.
Classification: LCC E312.66 J36 2027 | DDC 973.41092--dc23

Published in 2027 by
Norwood House Press
2544 Clinton Street
Buffalo, NY 14224

Designer: Rhea Magaro
Editor: Kim Thompson

Photo credits: Cover, p. 1 Rawpixel.com/Shutterstock.com; pp. 4, 6, 7, 9, 11-19 Library of Congress; p. 5 Benjamin Henry Latrobe); pp. 8, 10, 21 Wikipedia

Printed in the United States of America

CPSIA compliance information: Batch #CSNHP27: For further information contact Norwood House Press at 1-800-237-9932.

TABLE OF CONTENTS

Early Years

George Washington was born on February 22, 1732. He lived in this house in Virginia with his mother, father, and **siblings**.

When George was 11 years old, his father died. George went to live with his older brother Lawrence. They lived on a **plantation** called Mount Vernon.

At Mount Vernon, Lawrence helped George learn how to **survey**. When he was just 16 years old, George got a job and left the farm. His job was to survey the Virginia **frontier**.

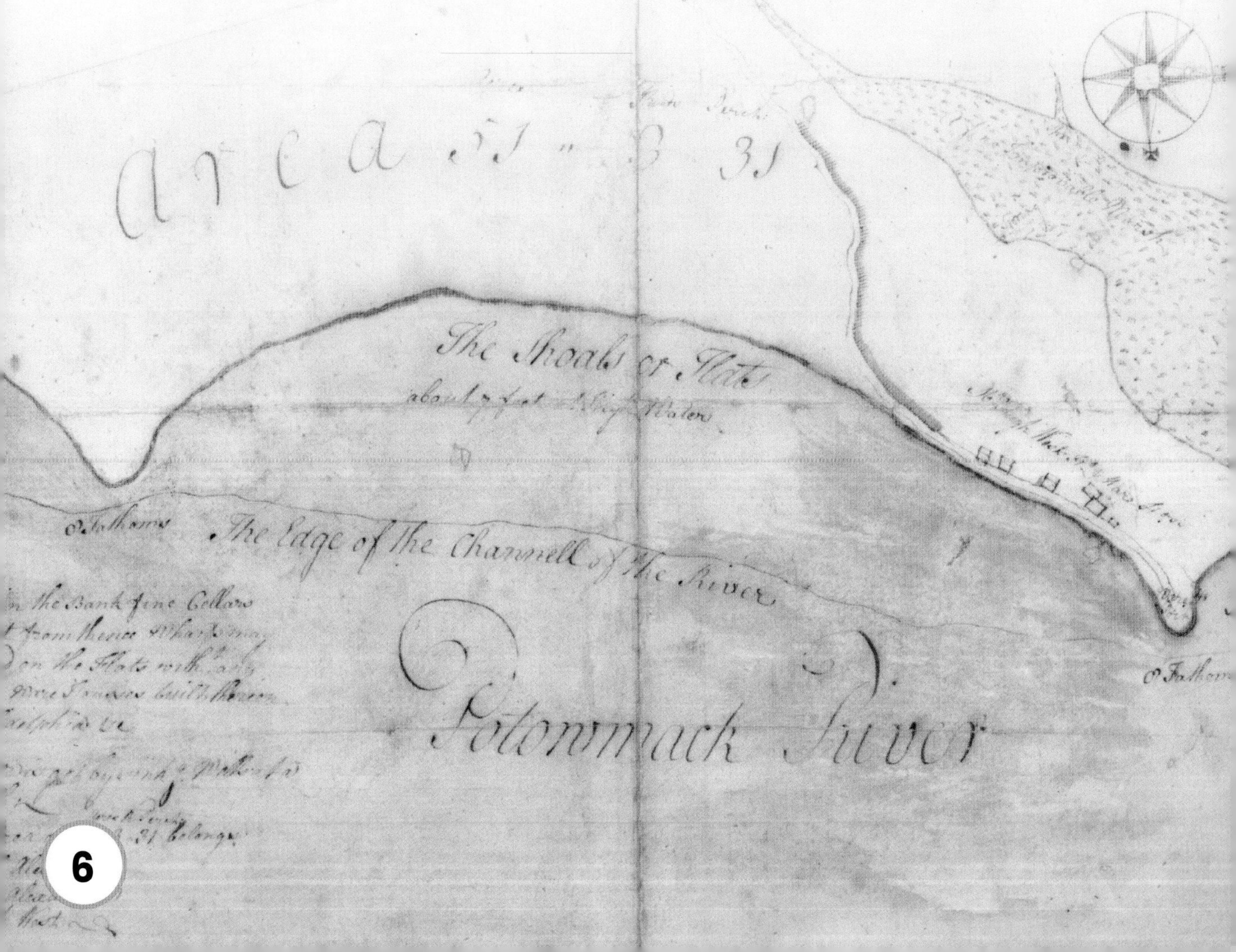

Building a Career

When he came back from surveying, George became a soldier. He fought in the French and Indian War.

George also became a **politician**. He was elected to Virginia's government when he was 26 years old.

He married Martha Dandridge in 1759.

George became a general during the American Revolutionary War. He led soldiers to fight against British forces for American **independence**.

American soldiers were poor and not well trained. General Washington showed he was a great leader by keeping the men together and fighting. On Christmas night in 1776, he led his army across the icy Delaware River to make a surprise attack on the enemy.

Presidency

In 1781, America won the war. It was a new nation. George helped write the United States **Constitution**.

It was time for Americans to choose their first president. They elected George Washington. He became the first president of the United States on April 30, 1789.

As president, there was a lot to do. George had to decide how the nation would form **treaties** with other countries. He had to choose people to advise him.

Each year of his presidency, George made a speech to give updates about the country. Presidents today still give this speech. It is called the State of the Union.

While he was president, George lived in New York, New York, and then in Philadelphia, Pennsylvania. He helped plan the city that was named after him and that would become the nation's capital, Washington, D.C.

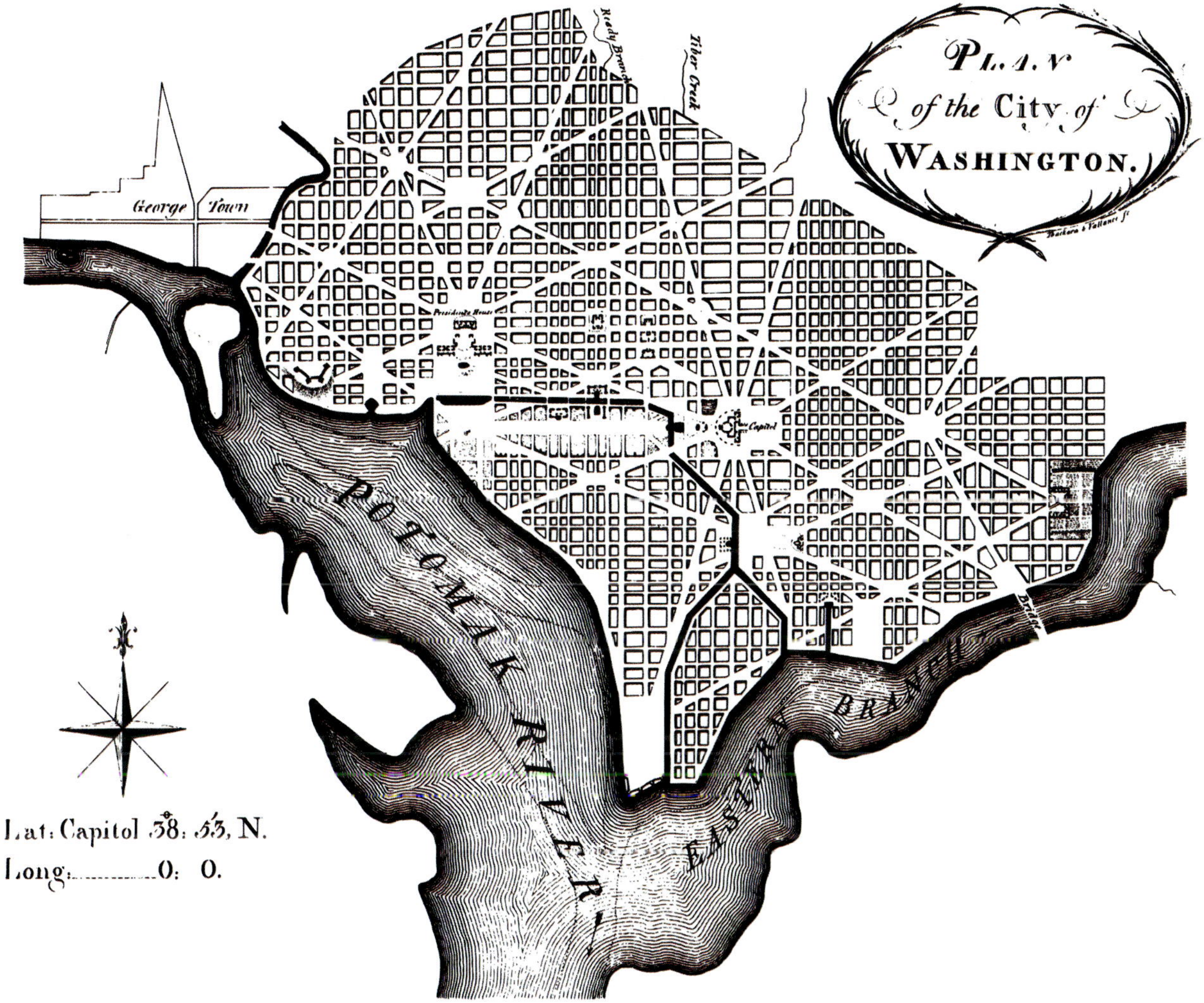
PLAN
of the City of
WASHINGTON.
George Town
Tiber Creek
Capitol
POTOMAK RIVER
EASTERN BRANCH
Lat: Capitol 38: 53, N.
Long:..........0: 0.

Later Life

Two **terms** as president were enough for George. He wanted to show that American presidents could give up their power to the next person elected. He peacefully stepped down in 1797.

George Washington died on December 14, 1799. He is remembered as a brave soldier, the first president of the United States, and a founding father who helped bring freedom to America.

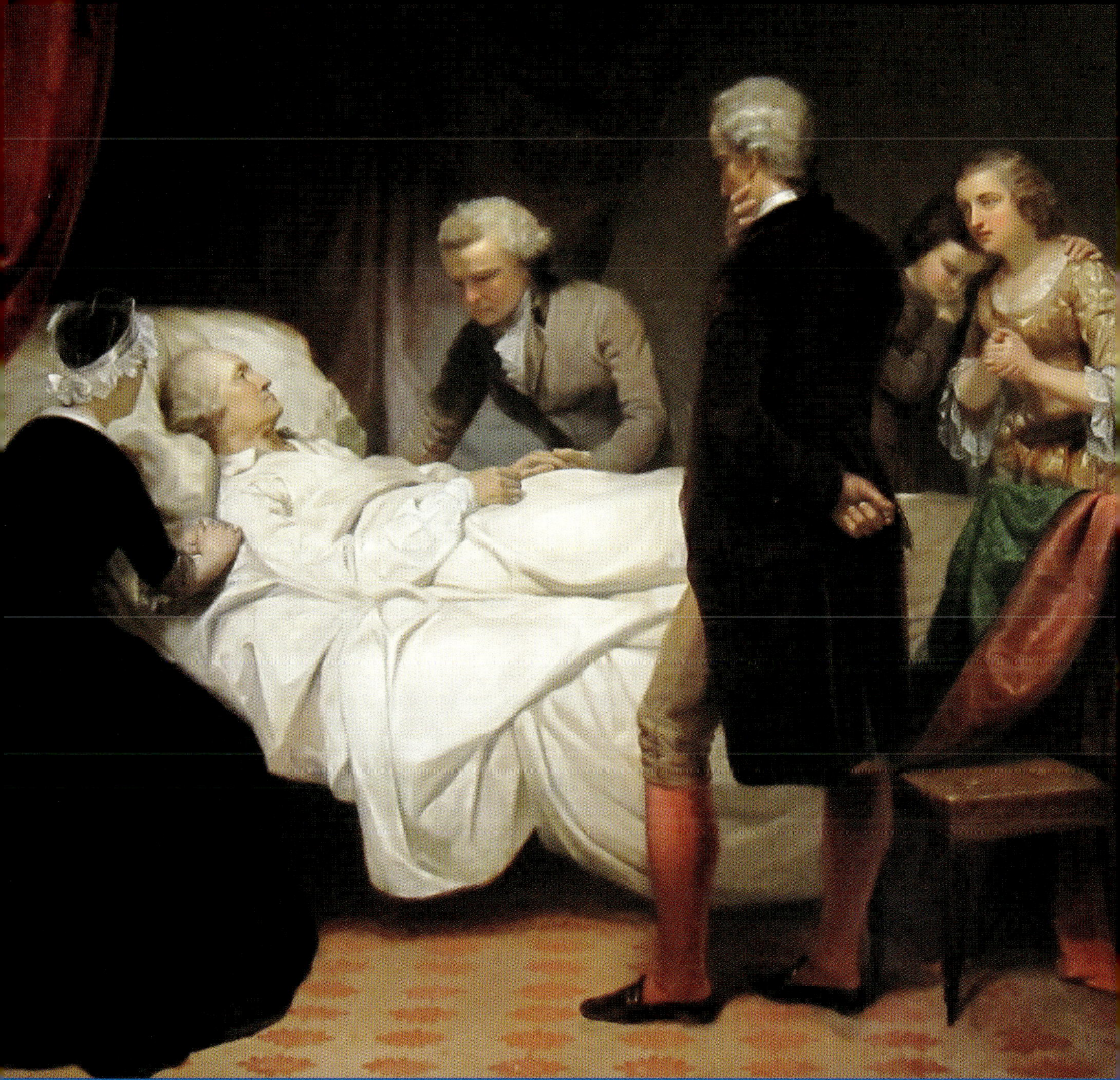

Glossary

constitution (kahn-sti-TOO-shuhn): a set of beliefs or rules for a group of people; the basic laws of a country

frontier (fruhn-TEER): the edge of a settled part of land; the far edge of a country where few people live

independence (in-di-PEN-duhns): freedom; self-rule

plantation (plan-TAY-shuhn): a large farm in a warm climate; workers on many American plantations, including Mount Vernon, were enslaved Black people—George Washington and many other early American leaders were enslavers

politician (pah-li-TISH-uhn): a person who is elected to serve in the government

siblings (SIB-lings): brothers and sisters

survey (sur-VAY): to determine the shape of land using measurements and math in order to create maps

terms (turmz): definite or set periods of time; American presidents are elected to terms that last four years

treaties (TREE-tees): agreements between countries

Thinking Questions

1. Why did George move to Mount Vernon?
2. How did George Washington show he was a great leader during the American Revolutionary War?
3. Give examples of what George Washington did as the first president.
4. What does it mean to "peacefully step down"?
5. What are some things that George Washington is known for?

Index

About the Author

India James writes about science, technology, math, and history for young readers. She loves learning new things while writing books. India lives in Ohio with her family.